THE SOCIAL INNOVATOR'S PLAYBOOK

*A COMPANY'S GUIDE TO CREATING
INNOVATION FROM THE BOTTOM UP*

*NICHOLAS D. TORRES
TINE HANSEN-TURTON*

SOCIAL INNOVATIONS
Journal, Institute & Lab

Copyright © 2017 by Nicholas D. Torres and Tine Hansen-Turton

All rights reserved. No part of this book may be reproduced in any form, or by any means, without written permission of the publisher. Company and product names mentioned herein are the trademarks or registered trademarks of their respective owners.

THE SOCIAL INNOVATOR'S PLAYBOOK

*A COMPANY'S GUIDE TO CREATING
INNOVATION FROM THE BOTTOM UP*

Visit www.socialinnovationsinstitute.com to download forms and templates.

AUTHORS' NOTE

We began our journey together in 2008. At the time, Eisenhower Fellowships was conducting an experiment in which two fellows were selected from different social sector industries to attend an international conference together. As a result, we learned much from each other, and forged a lasting friendship. Many conversations later, in 2009, we launched the Social Innovations Journal. We had a simple mission: to create a space for social sector leaders to share their ideas, and, in the process, to inspire others to dream and innovate too.

Over time, and based on reader demand, the Social Innovations Journal has expanded to include the Social Innovations Institute & Lab. Our mission is to teach and inspire civic and social leaders to better understand and undertake the process of innovative thinking and social entrepreneurship. In turn, this could solve many of the world's most pressing social issues. *The Social Innovator's Playbook: A Company's Guide to Creating Innovation from the Bottom Up* is based upon the knowledge gained through working with hundreds of social innovators over the years. Ultimately, we created a recipe for social innovators to dream and develop their social sector ideas, leading to successful launches and greater social impact. The key to our recipe for success lies in encouraging social innovators *how* to think, rather than *what* to think. Most importantly, this process is about helping individuals tap into their unique passions and motivations, leading to amazing new opportunities to test and launch their ideas.

Along our journey, we realized that the greatest opportunity to create social impact lies in creating an internal culture of social innovation within companies and organizations. This not only results in new services and products, but also improves existing infrastructure, ultimately leading to more effective programs and services.

We are extremely thankful to the hundreds of mentors and supporters that we have encountered through the years. Their encouragement and positivity has given us our own opportunities to pursue creative new ideas and dreams. For this reason, we proudly dedicate this book to giving back. We hope this guide inspires leaders and organizations to continue dreaming, taking on new and complex challenges, and striving towards a better future. Thank you for reading this book. We wish you great luck with your social innovations, and we hope that when you achieve success, you, too, will pay it forward to those following in your footsteps.

CONTENTS

Introduction...	*1*
Stage One: Idea Formation and Exploration...........................	*3*
Stage Two: Design Thinking and Rapid Prototyping.................	*9*
Stage Three: Financial Modeling and Raising Start-Up Capital...........	*19*
Stage Four: Scaling and Scaling Impact & System and Policy Influence	*29*
Stage Five: Execution Strategies	*35*
The Business Plan and Pitch Deck.......................................	*45*
Case Studies	*55*
a) Affordable and Accessible Healthcare in Urban Environments...	*57*
b) Social Mobility via College Completion............................	*63*
c) Early Literacy for Children with Learning Differences	*69*
Conclusion..	*79*
About the Authors	*80*
Social Innovations' Advisory Group.....................................	*82*

INTRODUCTION: A New Approach to Addressing Social Issues

The social sector in the United States has a rich history of connecting communities and individuals with vital resources to address our nation's most daunting social challenges. However, amidst today's increasingly competitive funding landscape and complex regulatory environment, the effectiveness and sustainability of traditional charities and nonprofits is often challenging. The public, as well as leaders in government and mission-aligned investors, are demanding new social models. They value systems which are cost-effective, financially sustainable, and adaptive to feedback; as well as those which have clear outcome accountability measures and potential for large-scale impact and systems change.

Social Innovators working in government, private, and nonprofit settings often find that their new ideas are stymied by organizational culture or funding limitations. A recent survey of nonprofit leaders conducted by Johns Hopkins University found that more than two-thirds of organizations developed at least one innovation in the past two years that they were unable to adopt, due to funding or other considerations.[1]

In the social sector, innovations are often new products or services. However, they can also be technical, managerial, or process-related constructs created in order to deliver services more effectively.[2] "Organizations tend to invest more in skills development and less in creativity, education, and training." This creates a natural barrier to innovation in the social sector.[3] As a result, even mature social sector leaders have no experience or training with the type of interactive opportunities offered through an innovation incubator process.

To ensure the social sector's evolution and viability, social innovation has emerged as an approach for business development, as well as a necessary catalyst for change. This approach combines social impact, financial accountability, policy and system change, and execution capacity to address some of society's most complex social issues.

The social innovation movement is gaining traction worldwide; in part because it combines the passion and commitment of the social sector with the business and financial savvy of the private sector. Unfortunately, there are few professional avenues available to support the creation, incubation, start-up, and scaling of new

---

[1] Johns Hopkins Office of Communications (2010). "Survey Reveals Widespread Innovation at Nation's Nonprofits."
[2] Seelos, C. and Mair, J. (2012). "What Determines the Capacity for Continuous Innovation in Social Sector Organizations?" *Stanford Center on Philanthropy and Civil Society.* Page 9.
[3] *Ibid*, page 24.

social enterprises. There are also far fewer capacity-building resources available to support even the most talented entrepreneurs within a company; many of whom lack formal social impact training, and do not have the knowledge and skills necessary to turn their ideas into positive social change.

As experienced social entrepreneurs, the authors of *The Social Innovator's Playbook: A Company's Guide to Creating Innovation from the Bottom Up* have developed a guide that balances creativity and ideation with mentoring, financial services, and access to human expertise capital. This comprehensive approach will help social entrepreneurs anticipate challenges and successfully execute their new ideas when the opportunity presents itself.

Practical Training to Inspire Entrepreneurial Mindsets: The model is built on the premise that innovation is a *process,* not just an end result. *The Social Innovator's Playbook: A Company's Guide to Creating Innovation from the Bottom Up* takes participants through a process of innovation which transforms leaders and their companies into smarter, sharper, better versions of themselves. The journey is an intensive, sustainable process in which innovators are invited to explore their ideas, test them, and adapt them for better outcomes. This process hones entrepreneurial and innovative thinking skills while developing, and eventually executing, new and improved business models. Through interactive guides and curriculum modules, participants from a variety of disciplines will imagine, refine, and pursue their own enterprises and innovations to solve some of the most challenging social issues to date.

Ultimately, this guide provides organizations and leaders with a framework for generating innovation from the people who know their target customers best. In the process, companies create and foster a culture of innovation, break down organizational silos, and ultimately triumph over their competition through improved products and services.

The Social Innovator's Playbook: A Company's Guide to Creating Innovation from the Bottom Up is divided into five stages which lead to the creation of a business plan and pitch deck. The five stages are: Idea Formulation and Exploration; Design Thinking and Rapid Prototyping; Financial Modeling and Raising Start-Up Capital; Scaling and Scaling Impact & System and Policy Influence; and Execution Strategy.

STAGE ONE

IDEA FORMULATION AND EXPLORATION

STAGE ONE: IDEA FORMULATION AND EXPLORATION

Before any social idea can be formulated, explored, or launched, it must take root in a fundamental belief. Successful social innovators are those who are driven by a thorough understanding of their personal passions and motivations. Without this vital understanding, the likelihood that their social idea will launch is significantly reduced.

Idea formulation and exploration asks you to better understand your social impact motivations and underlying inspirations. It translates them into a social impact "Why" statement, which becomes the primary selling point for your innovative ideas, social enterprise partnerships, and investments. A "Why" statement assists you in translating your ideas into concrete outputs, outcomes, and impact measures. Finally, examining your underlying inspirations and strengths helps you better understand your own leadership style, and aids you in assessing the leaderships styles of those you need to partner with along the way.

To begin this process, you must better understand your motivations and passions, and further explore the reasons you are dedicated to making a positive difference in the world. To do this, write your own "This I Believe Essay" (described in detail on the following page). Next, translate your story into a professional "Why" statement. Finally, consider which of your characteristics and traits match those of global, social entrepreneurs to better understand your strengths and weaknesses.

After completing this exercise, take a personality assessment to better understand your communication style. This will aid you in your understanding of the different types of communication styles, as well as increase your chances of being granted a pilot phase for your innovation.

Step 1: Complete your "This I Believe" essay. Guidelines are available in the following link: (http://thisibelieve.org/guidelines/)

"This I Believe" is an international effort to engage people in writing about their core values and beliefs; a project based on Edward R. Murrow's radio series from the 1950s. We understand how challenging this is, as it requires intense self-examination, and many will find it difficult to begin. To guide you through this process, we offer these suggestions:

- *Tell a story about you:* Be specific. Take your belief out of the ether and ground it in the events that have shaped your core values. Consider moments when your belief was formed or challenged. Think of your own experience, work, and family; what do you know that no one else does? Your story need not be heart-warming or gut-wrenching—it can even be funny—but it should be *real*. Make sure your story ties itself to the essence of your daily philosophy and the shaping of your beliefs.

- *Be brief:* Your statement should be between 500 and 600 words. That is approximately three minutes when read aloud at your natural pace.

- *Name your belief:* If you cannot name it in a sentence or two, your essay might not be about belief. Rather than writing a list, consider focusing on one core belief.

- *Be positive:* Write about what you *do* believe, rather than what you *don't* believe. Avoid statements of religious dogma, preaching, or editorializing.

- *Be personal:* Make your essay about you; speak in the first person. Avoid speaking in the editorial "we." Tell a story from your own life; this is not an opinion piece about social ideals. Write in words and phrases that are comfortable for you to speak in. We recommend that you read your essay aloud to yourself several times. Each time, edit and simplify it until you find the words, tone, and story that truly echo your belief.

Edward R. Murrow said, "Never has the need for personal philosophies of this kind been so urgent." We would argue that the need is as great now as it was 60 years ago.

Step 2: Watch Simon Sinek's TED Talk, "Start with Why." It can be accessed through the following link: (https://www.youtube.com/watch?v=sioZd3AxmnE)

After watching, consider the following questions:

1. What is the issue or social problem that you want to address?

2. Based upon the Golden Circle, write your social impact goal, starting with your "Why." Include a section on what success would look like in concrete terms if you achieved your social impact goal.

The Golden Circle

WHAT
Every organization on the planet knows WHAT they do. These are products they sell or the services

HOW
Some organizations know HOW they do it. These are the things that make them special or set them apart from their competition.

WHY
Very few organizations know WHY they do what they do. WHY is not about making money. That's a result. WHY is a purpose, cause or belief. It's the very reason your organization exists.

©2015 Simon Sinek, Inc.

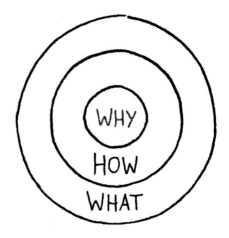

Step 3: Take a personality assessment. The following questionnaire will identify your personality as a type of bird (i.e. dove, owl, peacock, or eagle). Each bird has different characteristics associated with it, which will help you better understand your strengths and weaknesses as a communicator. You can access the test here: (http://richardstep.com/dope-personality-type-quiz/)

After receiving your results, consider the following questions:

1. What type of bird are you?
2. Do the characteristics associated with this bird describe you?
3. What traits do you associate with from the other types of birds?
4. What are the strengths and weaknesses of each bird?
5. How can you determine another person's personality bird type without having them take the test?
6. What strategy would you use to prepare a pitch to an eagle, peacock, owl, or dove?

Relationship Strategies

How to Identify and Communicate with the Four Behavioral Styles

Step 4: In David Bornstein's *How to Change the World: Social Entrepreneurs and the Power of New Ideas*, he lists the six character traits of successful social entrepreneurs: willingness to self-correct, willingness to share credit, willingness to break free of established structures, willingness to cross disciplinary boundaries, willingness to work quietly, and a strong ethical impetus.

Based on these character traits, answer the following questions on a scale of 1 (lowest) to 10 (highest):

1. Social entrepreneurs must often accept failure as a sign that they need to pivot or adapt their current innovation model. On a scale of 1 to 10, what is your willingness to self-correct? Why do you give yourself this ranking?

2. A social entrepreneur's true intention should be to make change happen, and sharing credit happens naturally through this process. On a scale of 1 to 10, what is your willingness to share credit? Why do you give yourself this ranking?

3. As constraints and bureaucracy in government and academia can hinder innovation, many entrepreneurs step outside of these institutions. On a scale of 1 to 10, what is your willingness to break free of established structures? Why do you give yourself this ranking?

4. Social entrepreneurs look for new ways to combine and use resources to achieve innovative, workable solutions to problems. On a scale of 1 to 10, what is your willingness to cross disciplinary boundaries? Why do you give yourself this ranking?

5. Entrepreneurs might spend years fine-tuning their ideas and influencing potential customers and stakeholders, with the understanding that recognition will come with time. On a scale of 1 to 10, what is your willingness to work quietly? Why do you give yourself this ranking?

6. Entrepreneurs are focused on their "Why," with no choice but to do the work they do, and they refuse to readily accept that something cannot be done. What is your ethical impetus?

STAGE TWO

DESIGN THINKING AND RAPID PROTOTYPING

STAGE TWO: DESIGN THINKING AND RAPID PROTOTYPING

Before your social innovation can be formulated, explored, or launched, you must perform a thorough analysis of the past and current strategies, models, and best practices used to address the social issue. Once you fully understand an issue's context, you can develop a unique social innovation that meets current deficiencies or challenges existing models.

This stage asks you to research the industry's current way of conducting business in order to determine your differentiation points. It also asks you to clearly define your target population to better understand their actual versus perceived needs, and, based upon an empathetic understanding of the target population's experience, to create a prototype to test on potential consumers. This testing phase will require adaptation and modification of the original prototype until you are comfortable with the product or service.

Step 1: Challenge Conventional Wisdom by Creating New Strategies; Modify the Rules of the Industry

Before developing an innovative idea that solves a complex social or environmental issue, you need to have an in-depth understanding of a problem and its context to understand what is or is not working, impact gaps, and how successful ideas might plug into existing efforts to solve these problems. This approach[4] asks you to acknowledge a range of possible interventions beyond starting a social business, such as expanding impact through government adoption, or franchising a current solution.

Watch the following video, which explains the Impact Gaps Canvas: www.oxfordglobalchallenge.com/video-using-the-impact-gaps-canvas/.

Using the Impact Gaps Canvas provided on page 14, answer the following questions:

1. What are the scope and effects of the problem? What are its causes? How has this problem changed over time?
2. What are the gaps in the landscape of the current solutions? What opportunities exist for increasing the positive impact of these solutions?
3. What are the current solution efforts, what are their models, and what future opportunities and threats do they pose?

---

[4] Gordon, M. and Papi-Thornton D. (2016). "Rethinking Business Plan Competitions." *Stanford Social Innovation Review*.

IMPACT GAPS CANVAS

CHALLENGE MAPPING
The scope & effects of the problem, its causes and how this problem has changed over time

IMPACT GAPS
Gaps in the landscape of the current solutions, and opportunities for increase positive impact

SOLUTIONS MAPPING
A map of the current solution efforts, their different models, and future opportunities and threats

---

CHALLENGE LANDSCAPE
How would you describe the challenge? Who or what is effected? How is it related to other issues

LANDSCAPE GAPS
Who or what is not being served, in the gap between the problem and the current solutions? What is missing that would further the collective impact of these efforts?

SOLUTIONS LANDSCAPE
What solutions are already being tried. Create a map of the current "solution" efforts by businesses, government, finance providers, and organizations, academia, media, local community groups, etc.

OBSTACLES TO CHANGE
What are the causes of this challenge and what is keeping it from changing? Who or what benefits from the current status quo?

UNADDRESSED OBSTACLES
What is missing or not working in each of these models for change? What are the unintended negative consequences of these efforts? What obstacles to change are still being overlooked?

MODELS FOR CHANGE
What different impact models are being tried? How are each of these models different and what parts of the problem do each of these models address?

HISTORY & FUTURE OF THE CHALLENGE
How has this problem or opportunity changed over time? What is the projected scope of the challenge in the future?

IMPACT OPPORTUNITIES
What are the specific key opportunities (market-based, regulation, research, education, partnership, etc) which can unlock future impact?

FUTURE IMPACT SCOPE & SCENARIOS
What new resources, opportunities, legislation, or changing demands are on the horizon which might impact the collective and individual solutions? What are possible future scenarios and how might these impact future efforts?

- - - - - - KEY INSIGHTS - - - - - -

CHALLENGE LEARNING LOG & OPPORTUNITIES
What resources have you used to understand the challenge? Who have you spoken with to verify your understanding of the challenge? Who else do you need to speak with to learn more?

What are the key lessons you learned about that are important for those who want to improve the landscape and impact of the solutions to your chosen challenge?

SOLUTIONS LEARNING LOG & OPPORTUNITIES
What resources have you used to understand current solutions which have been or are being tried? Who have you spoken with to verify and add to your understanding of the solutions landscape? Who do you need to speak with to learn more?

www.oxfordglobalchallenge.com/wp-content/uploads/2016/07/Impact-Gap-Canvas-eg-page-001.jpg

IMPACT GAPS CANVAS

CHALLENGE MAPPING
The scope & effects of the problem, its causes and how this problem has changed over time.

IMPACT GAPS
Gaps in the landscape of the current solutions, and opportunities for increase positive impact.

SOLUTIONS MAPPING
A map of the current solution efforts, their different models, and future opportunities and threats.

www.oxfordglobalchallenge.com/wp-content/uploads/2016/07/Impact-Gap-Canvas-blank-page-001.jpg

Step 2: Define your Social Impact Intentions

Before you can develop your innovative idea, you must develop a theory of change. A theory of change drives your entrepreneurial purpose by identifying the population targeted for service and the outcomes of your program's actions. An effective theory of change has meaning for stakeholders, clearly states how the program will be delivered, and can be measured or tracked over time.

Measuring outcomes is a necessary step in this process, and though it can pose considerable challenges, it is not as difficult as many might suggest. The primary difficulty lies in determining which data are needed, and establishing an efficient, accurate system for collecting them over time. To quantify and confirm impact, outcomes must be directly attributable to an organization's program or service. We provide the following explanations of short-term, intermediate, and long-term outcomes as created and defined by our colleague David Hunter. Use them as a guide to define your intended social impact.

Definitions[5]

- *Short-term Outcomes:* These are incremental changes that clients achieve in the course of their day to day program participation, and that can be thought of as "pathways" to the achievement of intermediate outcomes. New knowledge gained (e.g., knowledge of good parenting practices), new skills acquired (e.g., work readiness skills), and/or new behavior manifested (e.g., school attendance improved).

- *Intermediate Outcomes:* These are critical changes that clients achieve at key points in their program participation, culminating with criteria for deciding whether or not they are ready to be discharged from services. These conditions are those which you would view as necessary and sufficient in order to create a significantly higher likelihood that clients will achieve targeted long-term goals. For example, consistent use of good parenting practices, grade promotion culminating in high school graduation, or transition from antisocial to prosocial peer group.

- *Long-term Outcomes:* These are the results of program participation that serve as the ultimate basis for assessing a program's value to society. For

---

[5] Hunter, D. "Evaluating Organizational Impact and Outcome Measurement."

example, two years after program discharge, completion of an associate's degree program; one year after program discharge, success in keeping a job with promotion opportunities; two years post-discharge, not having been arrested for criminal behavior.

Ask yourself the following questions to better define your social outcome and impact goals:

1. How will this program change the lives of those who participate in it? Are these changes measured and monitored, sustained, linked to highly intentional staff efforts, and constitute what this program is held accountable for achieving?

2. What is the sequence of incremental changes that program participants or service recipients should pass through as they progress toward achieving the ultimate set of outcomes for which the organization or program is holding itself accountable?

3. Ultimately, what are your social outcomes and impact goals?

4. Are you realistically able to measure your social outcomes and impact goals? They must be measurable in order to include them in your final list.

5. Will you hold yourself publicly accountable (i.e. through use of a dashboard) to achieve these social outcomes and impact goals?

6. What measurement tools will you use?

7. What scorecard or dashboard templates will you use in order to report your social outcomes and social impact successes?

Step 3: Determine if your Innovation is Disruptive or Sustainable

During the innovation development phase, you need to understand whether your idea is a breakthrough, sustaining, or disruptive innovation. Your answer will determine your strategy and whether or not you are targeting existing or new markets. These terms are defined in detail here: www.digitaltonto.com/2012/4-types-of-innovation-and-how-to-approach-them/.

Watch Clayton Christensen discuss disruptive innovation in the following videos:
- http://www.claytonchristensen.com/key-concepts
- http://www.creativehuddle.co.uk/disruptive-innovation-explained

Sustaining innovations are typically created by established firms, improve established services, and meet the demands of mainstream consumers. *Disruptive innovations* are often created by new firms, do not perform at the level of established products, tend to be smaller and cheaper to use, and have greater value to new customers. *Breakthrough innovations* involve a paradigm shift where the problem is well defined, but the path to the solution is unclear; usually those involved in the domain have hit a wall.

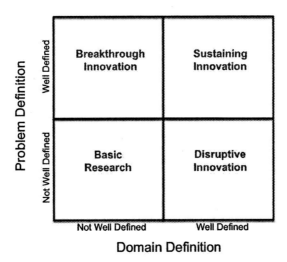

Step 4: Evolving your Social Innovation through Human Centered Problem Solving

Before creating a prototype of your service or product, you need to first attempt to understand your target group. Consider the following questions:

1. To whom are you in business to serve? Who is your target customer? Note that your customer is not your funder (i.e. the government, foundations, third-party payers, etc.). You need to sell exactly what your customer wants. In the social sector, many third-party payers, such as the government, are not in touch with what the customer wants. If you can find people who would pay even a small amount for your idea, you know your service or product is valuable.

2. Describe a customer profile. What are the attributes of people who would be willing to adopt your service or program? Think about whether this audience is aware that they need your product, if they will see the link between your work and the outcome, and how quickly they will see the benefit. Do your customers need to pay you directly, or will the benefit be funded for them?

3. What is the proposed value to the consumer? Think through the experience for your beneficiary. This is a crucial step, because the odds of success are low for social entrepreneurs unless you understand your end consumer.

Step 5: Evolving your Social Innovation through Rapid Prototyping

At this stage, you are ready to outline your social innovation. This prepares you for testing and confirming your idea's value within a target population. Keep in mind that, at this point, your innovation is based solely upon a theory, and that this theory is in its initial stages of development. Based upon target population feedback, it will organically evolve to a service or product that has great value to the target consumer.

The following steps will aid you in outlining your social innovation:

1. *Brainstorming:* List three to five practical and crazy ideas in a silent, three-minute brainstorming session. Share, in one to two sentences, the most practical, craziest, and best innovation.

2. *Selection:* Select one or two ideas to prototype. This should be quick; no more than one to three minutes. Create a visual aid (i.e. drawing or physical representation) for the target customer's "journey." If they received your service or product, what would their experience look like? Though labels are encouraged, avoid writing a long narrative. For example:

CUSTOMER JOURNEY MAP

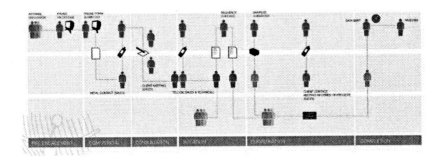

3. *Testing:* From an empathetic perspective, describe the consumer's experience. What is their state before, during, and after adopting your product or service? This should take the form of a narrative.

Next, in an organizational setting, test your idea by following the steps below:

1. *Test your prototype:* Partner with another group to test your idea. You will have three minutes to explain who you are (i.e. target market representative) and your innovation. The other team will then have two minutes to "think out loud" by providing you with honest feedback. The team members responsible for generating the idea must listen and take notes while avoiding the three Ds -- directing ideas about the innovation, defending ideas, and designing (asking, "what would *you* do?").

This is considered primary market research. When you do market research, consider that many people will tell you what you want to hear. Be sure to get to the root of what people want. Keep track of the assumptions you make as you develop ideas for your business or project, and update the list as you acquire new information. Note the source that allowed you to update your assumption (research report, expert, etc.). Remember to revisit these early assumptions as you continue your work, as they may inform changes you need to make in the future. Keep in mind:

- Social entrepreneurs identify problems that do not have obvious or lucrative solutions
- Social entrepreneurs need to create markets that do not already exist
- Social entrepreneurs work in areas that are inherently unstable due to emerging markets, volatile pricing, lack of governance, fragile infrastructure, and new technology

2. *Repeat step 1:* This time, allow the other team to present their idea.

3. *Adaptation:* Upon completion of this exercise, team members have five minutes to regroup and adapt their idea to test it on another group.

4. *Repeat:* Repeat this process with other groups until all team members are comfortable with the prototype of their idea.

5. *Pilot:* Take the adapted social innovation and test it on your target population.

STAGE THREE

FINANCIAL MODELING AND RAISING START-UP CAPITAL

STAGE THREE: FINANCIAL MODELING AND RAISING START-UP CAPITAL

Many social innovators start with the belief that their idea can only be launched through philanthropic investments, and that financial capital is required to launch an idea. This stage challenges you to determine if there is a recurring source of revenue that might lead to financial sustainability and scaling. It starts by asking you to understand how the industry is currently financed, and how to tap into existing sources of funding.

Once a revenue source is determined and expenses are projected, this stage helps you understand motivations for capital investments along the continuum of friends and family, crowdsourcing, family foundations, institutional foundations, direct government contracts, indirect government contracts, angel investors, mission-aligned foundations, and venture capitalists.

If your innovation does not have a source of recurring revenue, then this stage encourages you to do a Social Return on Investment (SROI) calculation.

Step 1: Determine your Revenue Sources

The goal for any social innovation is to determine a source of recurring revenue from which to construct a financial model. The first step in this process is to research the industry and determine who is getting paid for similar services. This essentially asks the question: are there organizations which currently receive financial resources in order to deliver a similar product or service? If so, what is their financial model?

The first potential revenue source beyond philanthropy or government grants is the consumer. Examples of other revenue models include: 1) using profits from a for-profit organization to finance the nonprofit; 2) operating a for-profit business in order to achieve the social impact goal (i.e. hiring ex-offenders to be the employees of a company); 3) creating a *pay-for-success social impact bond* in which private companies provide capital and the government pays back the private companies with interest if their social impact goals were achieved; 4) becoming a certified government or private entity which receives direct reimbursements; or 5) subcontracting with government authorized entities that tap into formula-based public financing (i.e. federally qualified health centers, charter schools, or colleges), but with less regulation.

Answer the following questions to determine your revenue sources:

1. What is your revenue model? Is there potential for multiple sources of revenue? Does your revenue model draw from how the industry is currently being financed?

2. Is your revenue model recurring? If not, can it become recurring?

Step 2: Create your Three-Year Financial Projections

To create a three-year projected financial model, you need to list your projected revenues and expenses over a three-year period. We recommend only constructing a three-year model because markets change rapidly, and projected revenues and expenses can alter significantly once the service or project is introduced to the target market. The purpose of developing a financial model is to not only demonstrate your knowledge of the industry, but also to speak to potential investors. A financial model provides valuable information and can answer investor questions regarding how much start-up capital is needed to fund your project. It also serves as a timeline for your projected break-even point and any potential surpluses.

Your goal is to create a spreadsheet with your initial revenue and expense projections, which can later be turned into a chart. Charts provide visualizations for your revenue growth, expenses, start-up capital, break-even point, and projected profits. They are extremely useful for start-ups, as they can be used to great effect in your pitch deck to show potential investors what your three-year financial projections look like. A sample spreadsheet is provided on the next page.

Spreadsheet Financial Template

			Year 1	Year 2	Year 3
Demand and Revenue Assumptions					
Cost Per Unit/Service					
Growth Assumptions for Program (narrative)					
Revenue Growth					
Number of Products Sold/Service Delivered x Cost					
Lost Revenue Projections					
REVENUES					
Staff Details					
Adm Staff ($00000 with Fringe)					
Financial Staff ($00000 with Base)					
Operational Staff ($00000 with Fringe)					
Adm Assistant ($00000 Base)					
Equipment					
Rent/Utilities					
Insurance/Audit					
TOTAL			0	0	0
Program/Service/Sales Details					
Director ($00000 with Fringe)					
Coordinator $(00000 with Fringe)					
Part Time Staff					
TOTAL			0	0	0
Marketing/Development Costs					
Development Costs					
Marketing Costs					
TOTAL			0	0	0
TOTAL EXPENSES			$ -	$ -	$ -
TOTAL LOSS/PROFIT			$ -	$ -	$ -

Consider your revenue and expenses, then answer the following questions:

Revenues

1. What are your projected, sustainable revenue sources?
   - Government contracts?
   - Government subcontracts with authorized or certified entities?
   - For-profit subsidization?
   - Direct consumers?
   - Individual donors?

2. Who is currently getting paid for this service? What is their financial model? How do you tap into this market?

3. Are you trying to identify and develop a new market of consumers? If so, what revenues do you project from this new market?

Expenses

1. What are your staffing (leadership, operational, marketing, service) costs? When will you start paying yourself?
2. What are the product development (i.e. prototyping) and marketing costs?
   - While you may not know exact costs at this stage of the project, you should do as much research as possible to ensure that your assumptions are accurate. These assumptions will be the basis for your fixed and variable costs, which you will use to make financial plans and estimate how much funding you will need.
   - If possible, avoid buying expensive, long-term assets during the start-up phase. They will deplete your funding and cause problems if your business does not succeed.

Step 3: Graphing your Three-Year Financial Model

By plotting your revenues and expenses, you should be able to answer questions as to when the model will be financially self-sustaining, when it will produce surpluses, and how much start-up capital is necessary to begin. Additionally, you will end up with a graph that communicates, in a visual manner, to investors the essentials of your business idea. This will help them determine whether or not they want to take a deeper look into your financial business model.

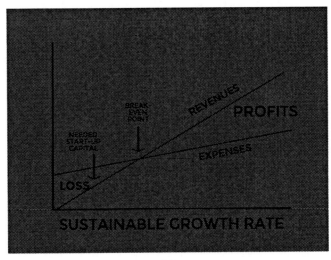

1. When is the model financially self-sustaining?

    - *Break-even point:* when the business transitions from losing money to making a profit; revenue and sales are large enough to cover costs. Use this to pinpoint how much you must sell every month to cover expenses.
    - Compare your total cost with your estimated revenue. Can you generate enough profit (or *surplus*, for a nonprofit) to cover operating costs, maintenance, and loan and investor repayments?
    - For nonprofits, factor in a small surplus, above expected costs, as a buffer against unexpected events and market changes.

2. When does the model produce surpluses?

    For long-run sustainability, a business must generate more cash than it spends. Consider these four places where you could produce a surplus, depending on the details of your project:

    - *Operating surplus:* when the organization brings in more funds than it spends on general operations.
    - *Asset replacement surplus:* calculate depreciation costs each year for assets including machinery, supplies, IT, or vehicles that will eventually wear out and need to be replaced.
    - *Inventory and receivables surplus:* set aside funds to offset delays in cash flow while you wait for customers or beneficiaries to pay you (if you offer a physical product).
    - *Debt and investment servicing surplus:* if you take out loans or have investments to repay, set aside funds for interest rates or investment returns.

3. How much start-up capital is needed?

    - *Start-up capital* is the gap between expenses and revenues until the model reaches the break-even point.

Step 4: Raising Start-Up Capital

Raising capital usually falls along a continuum with friends and family providing the initial capital, followed by crowdsourcing, family foundations, institutional foundations, angel investors, and then venture capitalists. Additionally, you can directly contract with the government through Requests for Proposals (RFPs); Subcontract with Government Authorized Entities; or create social impact bonds.

When your innovation is sustainable, consider whether your proposal is something new or merely an improvement upon existing services and products for existing consumers. This will affect the type of funding you seek.

Determine your best strategy to seek the start-up capital you need to launch your innovation. Where will you get your start-up capital? Who will provide the required seed capital (*e.g.,* angel investors, venture capitalists, foundations, government loans, etc.)?

Angel investors and venture capitalists will want to know the logic behind your start-up request. These sources of funding often seek *equity investments:* they invest money in high-growth, high-return businesses in return for a percentage of ownership. Because your success is uncertain, they might expect a high return in order to balance the risk. A good investor typically offers experience, industry knowledge, and connections. It is important that you research potential investors and make sure that they are a good match for you and your business before you strike a deal. Keep the following things in mind:

- Potential investors value those who can bootstrap. This is a lifestyle and mentality that shows investors that you would use their money well. If you have a large line item in your plan for your own salary, investors will be less likely to trust your judgment. The importance of *bootstrapping* (financing some or all of your business yourself) is that you can make investments in your business, which shows commitment to your mission and model.
- Advisors can become investors, because they feel they have helped build your business. Be sure to talk with people you trust early on.
- As the entrepreneur, you should be able to pitch and sell your idea in a compelling way. It is not sustainable to develop a business and scaling plan based primarily on who you will hire to do the work. Never forget the human element of your business: you are working

to make the world a better place for people who are desperate for positive change.

In the world of foundations, the first funder to support a new idea often gets a lot of credit. However, traditional foundations are typically unlikely to provide funding to create new nonprofits. Keep in mind:

- It may be advantageous to piggyback onto an existing nonprofit. This allows you to do your work while benefitting from their existing overhead structure.
- As a nonprofit, "free money" is counterbalanced by detailed grant reporting and accounting requirements.
- Nonprofits aren't able to scale (at least not initially) in the same way that for-profit businesses can.
- Consider functioning as a nonprofit-business hybrid. In this scenario, you create two branches within your model: one nonprofit and one for-profit. Though you pay taxes on your for-profit work, you are still able to channel funding towards your social innovation.

When looking at public funding opportunities, know that the government moves very slowly. It is risk-averse, and tends to have vendor relationships instead of formal partnerships. The social impact bond movement is attempting to change this culture, and although it is growing, its influence is limited.

Consider different types of loans:

- *Non-bank loans:* nonprofits and other entities have emerged to offer loans to socially-minded start-ups, which can have difficulty securing formal loans from banks.
- *Bank loans and credit lines:* typically require a business history, and, as a start-up, it may be necessary to personally guarantee the loan or acquire a cosigner.

Step 5: Social Return on Investment

Social Return on Investment (SROI) can be calculated when the business model is dependent upon philanthropy to demonstrate the social returns and impact. If your business model is not able to demonstrate income and profits, and you rely on philanthropic investments, then you should conduct an SROI to demonstrate the social return to society for their investment. This is also good practice for initiatives that have financial income and profits.

Follow these steps in order to determine your SROI calculation:

1. In concrete terms, what is the social outcome of your initiative? It must be something you can measure.

2. Determine the financial value of your outcome. Find a research study that indicates the value of your outcome, and cite statistics that support your cause. If a research study does not exist, create a logical financial value.

3. Determine your success rate regarding how many people achieve the desired outcome of your program or service.

4. Determine how many people would have achieved the outcome without the aid of your services.

5. Multiply the financial value of your outcome by the number of people who achieved the financial outcome.

6. Determine the number of years you take credit for the social impact.

7. Subtract the amount of money you spent achieving the financial outcome (i.e. any costs associated with your programs and services).

STAGE FOUR

SCALING AND SCALING IMPACT

&

SYSTEM AND POLICY INFLUENCE

STAGE FOUR: SCALING AND SCALING IMPACT & SYSTEM AND POLICY INFLUENCE

This stage challenges you to consider the growth and influence of your innovation after its initial pilot phase. This necessarily includes scaling, increased social impact, long-term strategy, and influence to systems and policy.

During this process, you must determine your scaling intentions and strategy. If your model has been successful, can it grow to include other target groups? Can it function in a different geographic location? Consider whether or not it is possible to scale your social impact without scaling organizational growth. The theory of disruptive innovation, which assumes that you will encounter resistance when you are successful, asks innovators to do a systems and policy analysis to determine what threats might impede their innovation from taking root and being successful. Once threats are identified, you can create new strategies for success.

Step 1: Scaling Intentions

Ask yourself the following questions to determine your scaling intentions. Then determine your strategy and how it might influence your financial projections:

1. How much growth do you see in your organization's future?

   - Evidence-based programs achieving valuable social impact can realistically plan to expand. In order to grow or replicate outcomes effectively, leaders must decide which aspects of the model will remain the same and which will change. They need to think about the leadership, financial, and organizational capacity of the organization, and how it might need to change in order to accommodate this growth.

2. Are there hazards to visibility?

   - *Visibility:* the price of success for your social enterprise. It helps you gain support but also inspires competition. In the world of social enterprise, competition is good for your beneficiaries because more people are positively impacted as their options and solutions increase.
   - *Attention and intervention from existing authorities*: as you grow, and especially as you disrupt existing structure and revenue streams, attitudes toward your business may change. You will likely attract

attention from existing authorities, who may require you to file for permits or meet certain regulations that did not apply to you before.
- *Vested interests shift from tolerance to attention or obstruction:* before you succeed, parties with a vested interest in your social impact area see you as a temporary annoyance. If you grow and begin to impact the systems they use, they may create new processes for you to follow or policies that make success more difficult. One example of this is increased rent and operating costs.
- *Labor force shift from grateful to organized:* in the early stages, people who work for you will be happy to have a job and make a social contribution. When you begin to succeed and scale, workers may start to organize, and will want to do better. This can result in your workers unionizing or organizing informally in ways that can ultimately complicate your organization.

3. Are you straining your ecosystem?

- When you expand, you may overburden your suppliers, which can hurt your product and beneficiaries. Pay attention to your suppliers and distributors.
- As a start-up, you are in a position of weakness with distributors. When you grow, distributors may increase prices or impose minimum quantities.
- *Shift in beneficiary behavior:* when you are new, beneficiaries are more willing to wait for the product. As you scale, they will raise their expectations and become less patient.
- *Losing trained employees:* as you invest in your employees through training and experience, they become more valuable. In turn, your competitors might seek out your employees and potentially offer them better opportunities within their own organizations.

4. What are your internal resource pressures?

- *Market shifts:* as you scale, you will segment your beneficiaries and focus on the most important ones. Now you must balance helping your beneficiaries with generating the necessary revenue to sustain the business.
- *Production shifts:* as you scale, it becomes more difficult to sustain your high output and quality levels. With increased volume comes increased production. This requires scaling on the part of scheduling and quality

control processes, which, in turn, requires trained management and staff.
- *Financial shifts:* when you grow, you will need additional liquid assets, such as inventory, which puts you under cash flow pressure. It is imperative that your accounting staff know how to manage finances for a growing business.
- *Workforce shifts:* inevitably, you will need additional people on staff as you scale. This requires more informed recruiting and training procedures. Take this opportunity to establish performance standards, train your best workers, and dismiss those who do not fit in well with the culture of the organization.

5. What are your management challenges?

- *Management shifts:* in the early stages, you supervised everyone who worked for you. When you grow, you will start thinking about recruiting, training, and supervising middle managers who perform well in your absence, as well as how to delegate tasks.
- *Moving away from the connected workforce:* scaling and adding a tier of middle management removes the personal management style of earlier stages of the business. Create a strategy to move employees away from direct interaction with you, and toward their new supervisors, so as not to diminish morale.
- *Conveying values:* create messaging and communication channels which illustrate the values of your company and your expectations for employees.
- *Delegating:* the demands on your time will increase as you scale. You have limited hours available for managing your organization, and should decide ahead of time which tasks to delegate to middle management.
- *Building finance and human resources:* as you shift from doing most tasks yourself to scaling, you will need to develop departments to manage finances and human resources issues such as staffing, training, and promotion.
- *Recruiting and training ahead:* scaling requires formal systems for recruiting and training employees *before* you need them. If you wait to hire help until the need is too great, you will be overburdened with training.
- *Financial planning:* scaling up calls for more strategic financial planning. Look at your funding needs and potential revenue sources

and continue to avoid purchasing expensive assets that unnecessarily increase your overhead.

Step 2: Scaling Impact as an Alternative Strategy

Read the following article: (https://ssir.org/articles/entry/whats_your_endgame)

Consider alternative scaling impact models and answer the following questions:

1. Can you scale your impact by means of influencing national, state, or local policy; consumer demand; and/or replication of the model?
2. Can you scale your impact through government adoption?
3. Can you scale your impact through replication?
4. Can you scale your impact through open sourcing or another, similar vehicle?

Step 3: Social and Political Analysis

Determine the potential implications of your social model on the social and political ecosystem by analyzing the sociopolitical factors which could impact your model. Develop a strategy to address them. Consider the following questions:

1. Are there existing policies in place that will impact the design, reception, or scale of this business model?
2. What social or political barriers exist? What might your other threats be?
3. Who will your investors and supporters be? Do they have specific social or political interests that might affect your working relationship?
4. Is the timing right to address your barriers and threats?

Three steps for identifying and addressing social and political considerations:

1. *Identify stakeholders:* your stakeholders are all of the people and organizations that will be impacted by your success, both positively and negatively. Think about their conflicts, potential reactions, and who you need to support you.

2. *Categorize your stakeholders:* allies, opponents, needed indifferents. Allies are those who benefit from your product and might support you; you should determine which allies have influence in the market for your project, and mobilize them. Opponents will be negatively affected by your project; if any opponents have influence in your market, you will need a strategy to address their concerns. Needed indifferents are people or organizations who are neither for nor against your project, but whose support or resources you may need (such as licenses or permits).

3. *Develop a strategy:* how will you engage your allies, manage opponents, and convert indifferents into supporters? Do you have the ability to influence these groups? If not, your project might not be viable in that location. Failing to account for your stakeholders will result in much wasted time, money, and effort.

   - Identify the response you need from a given stakeholder.
   - What issues are currently holding that stakeholder's attention?
   - Use your knowledge and skills: provide your allies with knowledge and capabilities that will help them (and hopefully grant you access to their network). Help opponents with potential issues to gain influence with them. Use your problem solving skills to improve an indifferent's position on an important issue in exchange for their support.
   - Do you have any physical or financial resources that could benefit your stakeholders, reward your allies, or win over opponents?
   - Use network connections – your allies and their allies – to mobilize supporters and help you manage your opponents.
   - Find a *safe haven:* this is the practical side of sociopolitics. You may need to identify a safe haven, or a protected position, where you can launch your project without immediate or strong opposition.
   - Create a diagram to map out your options for each stakeholder, and start with your strongest opponents. If you cannot move beyond them, you may need to redesign or re-envision your project.

STAGE FIVE

EXECUTION STRATEGIES

STAGE 5: EXECUTION STRATEGIES

Assuming you have been given the opportunity to pilot your social innovation, this stage challenges you to determine your strategy for success. This includes tapping into existing markets or creating new markets; conducting research on the competition and developing a strategy to compete; and conducting a self-assessment of your skills and competencies to identify and address deficiencies. Additionally, you must take this opportunity to assemble a strong leadership team, learn to manage natural fluctuations in business, and understand when to pivot. These are the key components of a successful organizational strategy, and can prepare you for seeking out partnerships, finalizing a pitch deck, and creating a narrative business plan.

Step 1: Market Development

Describe your strategy for penetrating the existing market, or to create a new one, by answering the following questions:

1. Is there an existing market for your innovation?

2. Brand identity is the personality of your business; it communicates who you are and why you exist, and it connects you with the interests and desires of your customers. Write down the characteristics that you believe your customer wants from your business. List key words that you would use to describe your business. Do they align?

3. What is the demand? Do you have enough supply?

4. What is your marketing strategy and what marketing outlets will you use?

5. How will you build a relationship with your customer? How will you get them to know and trust you?

6. How will you attract, keep, and increase your customer base over time? What is your price, and how will you sell your product or service?

7. List your key competitive factors; now list your competition's. Are they largely the same?

8. Are you prepared to fine-tune your message and market it based upon rapid validation?
    - Many emerging organizations pay special attention to social media platforms and the internet. These vehicles provide low-cost opportunities to fundraise, make connections, and promote the mission of your organization.
    - A marketing strategy requires clear objectives. What should each method of communication accomplish? Is it sharing the mission and its benefits, highlighting a leader, or marketing a new initiative internally?
    - *Cause marketing* attracts individual donors, often on a smaller scale, by inspiring them to support a social issue or need.
    - For efficiency, organizations that use social media for fundraising and cause marketing need to understand their audience. Finding the niche market for the program or service will help an organization reach its goals and raise awareness with fewer time and financial commitments.

9. Read about *Blue Ocean Strategy* as discussed in the following article: (http://www.blueoceanstrategy.com/what-is-blue-ocean-strategy/)
This strategy focuses on establishing and working within uncontested market space, capitalizing on new demand, reducing costs, and existing apart from competition. It is contrasted with the idea of the Red Ocean, which represents the traditional mindset around markets, competition, and business strategy.

Step 2: Organizational Competition and Partnerships Strategy

Analyze your competition, and identify your potential partners by answering the following questions:

1. Who are your closest potential competitors? What is the most competitive alternative already out there (i.e. who currently offers the best alternative approach to your product)? Are you attempting to deliver a substantially superior experience, or something only slightly different from an existing alternative?

2. Who and what is the competition? Government and nonprofit programs which subsidize your product or service can also be competition.

3. How are you different? If your solution to the problem does not seem to match existing programs, ask yourself if you can create something that is

substantially better. If not, it might be better to abandon your project than to waste valuable time and resources.

4. Analyze the most competitive alternative: who are they and how do they market their product?
5. How have similar initiatives marketed themselves? Have they succeeded?
6. Who are my organizational partners? What value do they add?
7. What are the legal and financial implications for a collaboration or partnership? How do I build partnerships, and what partnership models should I use?

Types of partnerships:

- *Collaboration:* involves minimal integration, does not change any party's corporate or legal arrangements, and may not require any written agreements.
- *Strategic Alliance:* organizations reduce costs and maintain independence by deciding to operate certain programs together. One approach involves sharing administrative services; the other involves combining programs through a contract or other formal agreement.
- *Corporate Integration:* alters legal structure so that all parties can maximize their strengths and successes. Examples include:
    - *Management services:* combines administrative functions
    - *Joint venture:* combines certain programmatic functions
    - *Parent-subsidiary:* combines both administrative and programmatic functions when a merger is not technically possible

Step 3: Define Your Leadership Competencies and Deficiencies

Consider the following questions:

1. What are your core strengths? What skills and competencies do you need to compliment your core strengths? Remember the results of your bird personality test.

2. Do you have the right leadership, management depth, skills, and expertise to execute your strategies?

3. Who are the people on your management team? Do they have the correct skill set to deliver as individuals and as part of the team?

   - *Selling skills*: you or someone on your team should be a persuasive, effective salesperson who can secure the support you need while addressing and mitigating the concerns of potential customers and beneficiaries.
   - *Operating skills*: a team member in charge of operations must be able to manage planning and scheduling while maintaining output and quality. An effective operations manager pays attention to detail at all stages of the process, always with an eye on quality.
   - *Accounting and cash management skills*: cash flow pressure is common in the start-up stages, even if the business is quickly succeeding and growing. When your demand is growing, you need to build up your inventory ahead of time.
   - *Negotiating skills*: there will be negotiations critical to launching your business; if a negotiation fails, it can damage your performance and potential for success.
     - When negotiating from a position of weakness, know what the worst possible deal for your business would be. You need to establish a line beyond which you walk away; otherwise you might concede too much and damage your business.
     - Make sure both parties in the negotiation have clearly specified who is responsible for actions and activities as part of the deal.
   - During start-up, *avoid hiring full-time staff members*. Pay per task and create contracts until you are stable and successful enough to hire. Managers can be too expensive at the outset.
   - Everyone on your team should know the break-even metrics, and must be prepared to work harder as deadlines approach.
   - *Never compromise quality* in the early stages of your enterprise. If your first customers and beneficiaries – who have taken a risk in doing business with you – see you as unreliable or delivering a less than perfect product, your business may fail. When establishing a new product or service within a new market, it is helpful to spend time with your customers and establish criteria to determine the quality of your product.

- *Never forget morale.* When you meet a goal or achieve a marker of success, no matter how small, congratulate your team and share the good news.
- Continue to *track and update your list of assumptions*, even as the business grows. It is easy to lose sight of these thoughts and ideas from the earliest stages, and end up relying on an initial assumption that proves to be false or misleading.

Step 4: Managing the Potential Upsides and Downsides

Social enterprises are more likely to fail than to succeed, and it is important to know what failure means. The ability to recognize when things are not going well is crucial to avoiding significant financial loss to a failing business.

Describe your strategy to adapt and pivot. How will you define failure?

1. *Define failure.* Before you launch, decide what failure means based on the minimal amount of revenue and delivered social impact in a certain timeframe. Below this marker, you would agree to disengage from your business and devote your energies to a different project.

2. *Monitor sociopolitics.* Track your stakeholders, share positive impacts, and refer to your strategy to watch and deal with negative impacts. The positive social impacts you achieve will help you mobilize allies and indifferents, and win over opponents.

3. *Preplan for disengagement.* If the project fails, plan how you will disengage from it. While this process is counterintuitive, there is a high probability that your innovation may fail. In the event of your exit, you want to leave your beneficiaries in the best possible position, and leave behind as small a footprint as possible.

4. *Monitor for second-order effects.* These are consequences, intended or not, of your business succeeding. The effects can be positive and helpful to society, or negative. In the latter case, your shortcomings can be employed by your opponents to justify obstructing your business.

5. *Redirect your project or launch a different one.* Even if you are motivated by altruism rather than by profit, looking for ways to address social issues forces

you to be careful about your resources. In the event you cannot achieve a growth profit through your business, you may be able to operate as a self-sustaining nonprofit, or a nonprofit that has some revenue but needs occasional funding.

Step 5: Define and Develop your Entity Type and Legal Considerations

1. Keeping the law in mind: all businesses and social enterprises are responsible for following certain laws and regulations. Selecting your start-up entity type is one of the most important decisions you will make.

   - *Sole proprietorship:* you and your business are the same, with profits and losses reported via your individual tax return. You are liable for any debt or legal action. This structure is inexpensive but carries personal risk.
   - *Partnership:* two or more people own the business. Each makes contributions, and each shares in profits and losses.
     - *General partnership*: everything is equally divided unless specified otherwise in the partnership agreement.
       - Pros: inexpensive to form, shared commitment, pooled resources, encourages complementary skill sets, joining the partnership can become an incentive for employees
       - Cons: shared liability, potential for disagreements among owners, shared profits, must pay self-employment tax
     - *Limited partnership*: there are general partners and limited partners, who are protected from assuming personal risk and have little management authority; they are often paid a return on their investment.
     - *Limited liability partnership*: partners' personal assets cannot be used to satisfy debts and liabilities of the business. In some states, this type of agreement is only available to certain professions.
     - *Limited liability company* (LLC): protects owners from personal liability, because debts and legal claims are restricted to business assets only. LLCs are taxed at the individual level, so members report earnings on their personal tax returns. It requires additional legal work and more start-up costs than partnerships, but offers beneficial liability protections.
   - *Cooperative:* a group of people who decide to cooperate and work together to be more effective and efficient. Members have a common need, and agree to jointly address a need through one strategy. They

vote equally, and are responsible for making sure the cooperative functions.
- ○ Pros: fewer taxes, opportunities for government grants, group purchasing power, can exist even if membership grows or shrinks, democratic
- ○ Cons: less attractive to investors because of members' equal voting rights, all members must participate and pull their weight for the business to operate
- *Corporations:*
  - ○ *C Corporation*: controlled by a board of directors and owned by shareholders. A C Corp is a separate entity from its owners and is taxed accordingly. While it can raise capital from selling stock and is an attractive employment option, it is time-intensive, costly, and complex to start a C Corp.
  - ○ *S Corporation*: like a C Corp, an S Corp operates separately from its owners and assumes all risk. However, taxes on profits and losses can be passed to shareholders. The S Corp has strict operating procedures and must compensate shareholders who perform services.
- *Social Entities:* combine aspects of nonprofits and other socially-minded businesses with those of for-profit businesses. The social mission is tied to the legal structure. They are not recognized in every state.
  - ○ *Low Profit Limited Liability Company* (L3C): gives companies the flexibility to raise capital for social or charitable purposes, while allowing them some profit to use as returns to investors. The IRS has issued very little guidance on tax obligations for L3Cs.
  - ○ *Benefit Corporation* (B Corp): corporation created for a social or environmental reason.
- *Nonprofit and other tax-exempt organizations:* though filing for tax-exemption is a long and complicated process, this may be the best fit for certain types of businesses. Nonprofits follow specific rules about raising and using money that differ from for-profits. It is important to remember that for-profit businesses can have social missions.

2. A brief overview of other legal considerations related to starting a new entity:

   - *Incorporation and licensing:* you may need to file paperwork with the state to register your business name and be legally recognized. Various licenses and permits may be required at the local, state, and national level depending on the nature of your businesses and product.
   - *Intellectual property:* a means of legally recognizing new and unique ideas, inventions, or processes. Examples include:
     - *Patent:* protects an invention. Provisional patents can quickly help you claim your idea for a year at a lower cost while you go through the official patent process, which is more expensive and takes considerable time.
     - *Trademark:* protects a brand -- specifically words, names, symbols, sounds, and colors -- that differentiate your goods and services from other companies.
     - *Copyright:* protects a creative work, published or unpublished, such as literature, drama, music, and art.
     - *Trade secret:* protects confidential information, such as a formula, process, design, pattern, or compilation. There is no filing required, but businesses must take care to limit access to the information they do not want disclosed.
   - *Hiring staff:* you must follow legal procedures if you decide to hire. Consult the Small Business Administration for a full list of tasks to complete. Consider the following:
     - You must obtain an *Employer Identification Number* (EIN) from the IRS, which is essentially a social security number for your business.
     - *Records for tax withholding:* your employees must fill out W4 forms to be sent to the IRS, and submit *W2* forms for each employee annually. Specific reporting requirements can vary by state.
     - You must submit the form *I-9*, which verifies that employees are not working in the U.S. illegally.
     - *New Hire Reporting Program*: employers must report new hires and rehires to a state directory.
     - *Workers' compensation insurance*: businesses are obligated to carry this insurance, either through a private carrier, on a self-

insured basis, or through the state workers' compensation insurance program.
- *Required notices*: employers must post notices in the workplace informing employees of their labor rights.
- *Taxes:* employers who pay wages are subject to income tax withholding, Social Security, and Medicare.

3. *Staying out of trouble*: important practices for responsible managers
    - Separate personal and business expenses, even if you are a sole proprietor. This will allow you to track your funds and minimize trouble. Use a different bank account and credit card for your business, and pay yourself using this account as needed.
    - If you set up any contracts or partnership agreements, ask a lawyer to review them. When you sign documents, be clear about whether you are signing as an individual or as a representative of your business.
    - Get legal advice: talk to a lawyer, or, ideally, ask a lawyer to be part of your advising team.
    - Use a calendar to track deadlines and required government filings.

THE PITCH DECK

&

BUSINESS PLAN

THE PITCH DECK AND BUSINESS PLAN

THE BUSINESS PLAN

The purpose of the business plan is to produce an overview document of your social innovation that you can leave with potential partners, investors, and team members. The business plan narrative should include an **Executive Summary** and an overview of the **Opportunity** that you are offering (including information on the social issue, its context, current best practices, gaps, and competition). Additionally, it should include a summary of your **Innovation, Idea, or Model** with corresponding information about its target market, model logistics (with a visual, if possible), and a unique value proposition. Your **Organizational History, Team Competencies, Partnerships, and Financial Plan** are also crucial elements of your business plan, and should include a three-year financial statement; financial statement narrative, social return on investment (if seeking philanthropic funding), and an **Execution Strategy** with milestones and benchmarks. Finally, many business plans incorporate target goals and dates, as well as a list of potential investors.

Step 1: Create a cover page that includes your company logo, tagline, prepared date, and contact information.

Step 2: Complete a three to five page business plan narrative by using the following business plan template. Add or delete sections as needed so that all of the information you include is relevant to your particular project. In other words, use this as a guide to help you draft a concise business plan to provide your target audience with the essential information they need to invest or partner with you.

Business Plan Template

Executive Summary

Executive summaries should include information regarding the social issue, its context, solutions, target market, and solution summary. It also includes information about needed start-up capital and three-year financial plan.

Opportunity

Social Issues and Context

In more detail than you provided in your executive summary, provide information about the problem you are solving. What do your customers need? Do they need a better product, or a cheaper service? Do they need better access to potential solutions? Describe why this problem is worth solving, and why customers will want to buy from you.

Current Best Practices and Gaps

Provide additional detail about your product or service. What are current best practices, and what are their limitations? What is unique and special about your company that will set it apart from the competition?

Competition

Describe your current competition. What products and services are people using instead of yours? How are you different?

Innovation, Idea, or Model

Target Market

Describe your key customers. Who are they, and what are their key attributes? If your solution targets multiple *segments* (customer groups), describe each group here. If you can, include details about how many people are in each segment, and how large the total market is.

Model Logistics

Describe your model with the aid of visualizations and a short narrative. What will your customers' journey look like? Provide enough information that your reader will understand how and why your model works.

Advantages and Unique Value Proposition

Explain why your product or service is better than others. Be sure to describe any competitive advantages you have, such as a patent or other unique component to your business.

Team Competencies and Qualifications

Overview

Use this area to specify your organizational history. Identify your company's legal structure; is it a nonprofit or for-profit organization? If it is for-profit, is it a sole proprietorship, a partnership (LLC or LLP), or a corporation (S or C type)? Describe your current structure and why it best suits your cause and model.

Team

Management Team

List the members of the management team, including yourself. Describe each person's skills and experience and describe their role in the company. At this stage, it is okay if you do not have a complete management team yet. Make sure to identify deficiencies in your team and explain how you will address them over time.

Advisors

Describe any mentors, investors, former professors, industry or subject-matter experts, knowledgeable friends or family members, small business counselors, or others who can help you as a business owner.

Financial Plan

Forecast

Key Assumptions

Describe how you formulated the values in your financial forecast. Did you project your revenue based on past results, market research, your best guess at how many people will utilize your service, or some other method? What kind of growth are you assuming? What are your key hires and notable expenses? What level of profits, by year, do you expect to generate?

Include your *Three-Year Financial Projections Spreadsheet* to provide an extra level of detail.

Describe your financing plans. Are you investing your own money in the business? Do you have a credit card or line of credit? What other types of funds — personal or business loans, equity investments from others, etc. — do you expect to receive and when? It is okay if you do not have the full detail of your future financing worked out yet. Instead, explain what you already know, and how you plan to address the remaining details in the future.

How much do you need in start-up capital? When do you break even, and when will you have surpluses?

Execution Strategy

Marketing & Sales

Marketing Plan

Explain how you plan to spread awareness about your product or service to your target market(s). Will you use advertising? Are you are developing a content marketing strategy? Whatever your marketing plans are, describe them here.

Sales Plan

If your company relies on sales people to close sales deals, you need a comprehensive sales plan. Your sales plan should explain how you convert people who express interest in your product or service into paying customers. If you are opening a food truck, for example, this section might be less important, and you might consider removing it. However, if you are starting a sales-heavy business with enterprise software or a car dealership, you need to document how you will nurture leads and close deals.

Operations

Locations & Facilities

Describe your company's physical location(s). This might be your office, store locations, manufacturing plants, storage facilities; whatever is relevant to your business. How much space do you have available, and how well will it meet your current and future needs?

Technology

Describe any important software, hardware, or other information technology that you use now, or plan to use later, to operate your business.

Equipment & Tools

List any specialty equipment that you have, or plan to acquire, in order to do your work. This is an important component of the business plan for many industrial companies.

Milestones & Metrics

Milestones

List your key milestones and dates. If you have already accomplished key goals for your business, list them here as evidence that your business is gaining traction. This is vital to proving that your services are attracting positive attention from potential customers.

Key Metrics

Explain which performance metrics are most important for understanding how your business is doing. What does success mean for you, and how will you know it when you see it?

THE PITCH DECK

At this point, you will have developed a five to seven minute pitch based on your social innovations model.

Your organization should assemble three to five senior executives to serve on a judging panel. The role of the judging panel is to ask questions to determine which social innovations the organization will adopt and execute. The entire organization should be invited to watch the pitches, as this encourages a culture of innovation and demonstrates the company's investment in innovative thinking.

Each team should be given five to seven minutes to pitch their innovation with an additional five to seven minutes to answer questions from the judges.

At the end of the presentations, the judges should meet and discuss the pitches. Judges should provide general feedback to all the pitches and announce with social innovations they would like to invite for additional consideration and potential investments.

Develop a presentation to effectively market your business plan.
Review the "11 Essential Slides" article here: (http://articles.bplans.com/what-to-include-in-your-pitch-deck/)

After you finish reading the article, take a moment to consider these questions:

1. What is your presentation style, and what is your approach to communication?

2. Start developing a pitch to attract interest from potential partners and communicate your mission. Put the most important information at the beginning of your presentation.

3. Utilize storytelling as a tool for success: it makes a personal connection with your audience and makes it easier for the listener to relate to you. Be sure to use your own words and speak clearly and concisely.

4. Consider your audience. Are you pitching to potential investors? Are you trying to attract potential customers?

5. Be concise, and practice your pacing and delivery.

6. Bring a product or demonstrate the service if you can. Use screenshots instead of relying on live technology.

7. Share the attributes of your idea that make it unique.

8. Think ahead about potential questions, and be prepared to answer them.

9. Use the following roadmap for planning your pitch in this order: first describe the problem, then the customer, competition, solution, benefit, advantage, message, distribution, revenue, start-up needs, costs, etc.

10. A pitch is an opportunity to get good advice; be sure to ask for feedback from anyone who declines to invest. You can learn as much from your failures as you can from your successes.

11. Incorporate details in your pitch that speak to your expertise, professionalism, and credibility. As an entrepreneur, you are selling yourself along with your product.

12. Your slide presentation and other visuals should not be a crutch; they should support your pitch. Consider setting up automatic transitions for your slides to keep your presentation moving forward.

13. Think about the bottom line. Measurable impact goes hand in hand with your altruism and desire to make a difference.

CASE STUDIES

In the following chapter, we provide three social enterprise case studies which demonstrate the innovation creation process from beginning to end. At the beginning of this book, we noted that the greatest challenge you will face in launching your new ideas will be developing a consumer market and selling to existing institutions. While writing this book, we realized that new innovations have a better chance of launching and succeeding if they are supported by existing structures and organizations. Even though our case studies are social innovations created and designed outside of existing institutions, we believe that, if organizations adopt the same practices and behaviors described above, they have a greater chance of achieving a positive social impact.

The case studies examined on the following pages focus on the three social sector industries that make up the majority of social innovations work: healthcare, K-12 education, and social mobility. We present these examples in their developmental framework stages, and follow their evolution using the steps outlined above.

ACCESSIBLE AND AFFORDABLE HEALTHCARE IN URBAN ENVIRONMENTS

Stage One: IDEA FORMULATION AND EXPLORATION

Step 1: Defining our "Why"

Having worked for decades in impoverished urban communities, we (your authors) knew that accessible, affordable, and quality primary healthcare was hard to find in low-income communities. We decided to tackle this issue by focusing on young populations. Our inspiration stemmed from the vision of one of our colleagues who dedicated her professional life to ensuring that students were healthy enough to learn. We also knew, from existing data sets, that poor health was a substantial barrier to succeeding in school. Although this issue had no personal impact on us, we were motivated by another person's "Why" to help launch this social enterprise.

Our collective belief was that lack of access to healthcare should not be a barrier to students' success, and that all children should have access to primary and preventive healthcare. From this belief, we began to look for innovative models which would bring primary healthcare *to* the individual, which was in direct opposition to the current system, in which individuals must seek out primary healthcare.

Stage Two: DESIGN THINKING AND RAPID PROTOTYPING

Step 1: Challenging conventional wisdom which modifies the "rules" of the industry

In researching alternative models, we took the lead from the Convenient Care Association (CCA), of which Tine was a Founder and Executive Director. CCA is the national trade association of companies and healthcare systems which provide consumers with accessible, affordable, quality healthcare in retail-based locations. The Convenient Care Association's members (such as CVS Caremark, Walgreens, Walmart, and others) had already begun tackling the issue of accessible primary healthcare by opening clinics, staffed by nurse practitioners and physician's assistants, in community-based, retail settings with convenient locations and hours. Harvard Professor Clayton Christensen had coined them a disruptive innovation, as they turned primary care upside down, and showed the existing medical establishment that healthcare could fit into people's busy schedules. Again, this was in direct opposition to traditional care in which people must schedule visits and wait long hours to be seen. Retail clinics, on the other hand, provide immediate relief to patients from a qualified healthcare provider without a prescheduled appointment. In the time since the first Convenient Care Clinics (CCCs) opened in 2000, the Convenient Care industry has grown rapidly. Today there are more than 2,400 such clinics in operation in 43 states.

In our research, we also examined school-based health centers that have long been recognized for their critical role in improving health and academic outcomes among vulnerable children. This impact is best achieved through partnership with the student's home medical home center, particularly for children living with chronic conditions. School-based health centers (SBHCs) are primary care centers located within schools to provide preventive and acute primary care to students. Approximately 75% of these centers also provide mental health services. Nearly 40 years of research support the positive impact that school-based health centers have on student achievement and wellbeing, as well as substantial cost savings to society. School-based health centers reduce absenteeism, emergency room utilization, hospitalization, and Medicaid costs; particularly for children with chronic health conditions like asthma. Asthma management in school-based health centers decreases hospitalization rates by up to 75 - 85%, and improves the use of peak flow meters and inhalers.

Numerous studies have demonstrated the effectiveness of SBHCs in engaging youth in mental health services. In studies of SBHCs service utilization, mental health counseling has been repeatedly identified as the leading reason for visits by students. One study found that "inner-city students were 21 times more likely to make mental health related visits to school based health centers than to community health centers." This reinforced the need for integrated, school-based healthcare in Philadelphia, where 33% of children live below the poverty line, 41% of children are overweight or obese, 23% of children have asthma, and the on-time graduation rate for public school students is just 61%.

We saw opportunity in both models, and began to think about how we could combine them to provide access and immediate relief to school children so their education would not be compromised.

Step 2: Design Thinking and Rapid Prototyping

Research showed us that, despite the overwhelming success of school-based health centers, financial sustainability and scaling was a challenge. Unfortunately, SBHCs do not fit into our education or healthcare funding models. They were financial loss leaders and mostly grant-funded.

Borrowing, instead, from the retail clinic model, our innovation was to place a nurse practitioner (in lieu of, or in addition to, a school nurse) into a school setting. Registered Nurse Practitioners are able to bill Medicaid and health insurance companies, and have the qualifications necessary to provide preventive, primary care. We theorized that if we provided primary healthcare in schools (the setting where students spend a significant part of their day), we could prevent poor health conditions and better manage chronic health conditions, such as asthma.

First, we defined the goals of School-Based Health Centers. Their primary mission was to: 1) improve healthcare access, outcomes, and cost; and 2) decrease school absenteeism among low-income school students.

In order to get the first pilots launched, we partnered with two charter schools in low-income Philadelphia neighborhoods. Each of these schools' leaders recognized the impact of poor health on academic outcomes. For example, they recognized that asthma remains the leading cause of absenteeism from school.

Our initial design installed a nurse practitioner in place of the school nurse in the pilot schools. Based on student needs and increased demand of the nurse practitioner's reimbursable services, however, this model evolved to include a full-time Licensed Practical Nurse (LPN) as well as a part-time Nurse Practitioner. In combination, the nurses were able to serve students in each school with first aid, medication administration, student health screenings, and primary care for acute sick visits, preventive care, and chronic care management as appropriate. Primary care was provided in collaboration with a primary care provider (PCP), to be communicated by the program's cloud-based electronic medical record (EMR) for documentation, billing, and parent and provider communication. High school students were also able to receive confidential, reproductive health services for sexual health education, non-hormonal birth control (condoms), screening, and treatment for sexually transmitted infections. Dental and vision partners provided ancillary screening and clinical services.

Further model developments separated non-billable school nursing as a service that could be delivered by LPN School Nurse Assistants. These assistants could script and enable the work of the Nurse Practitioners to deliver the following structured interventions:

- Asthma screening for all students at risk for new diagnosis via demonstrated allergies and skin conditions
- Asthma care management for all diagnosed asthmatic students via spirometry for lung function assessment, medication management, student and parent education, and PCP collaboration
- Risk assessment and intervention as indicated for all students via the American Academy of Pediatrics' Bright Futures tool, the Patient Health Questionnaire (PHQ,) and the Pediatric Symptom Inventory (PSC) for mental health screening
- Reproductive health assessment, screening, and treatment as indicated in the high schools
- Obesity intervention for students screening overweight or obese (44% in the last school year)

Stage Three: FINANCIAL MODELING AND RAISING START-UP CAPITAL

In researching who was currently getting paid to deliver this service, we realized that schools were spending between $45,000 and $75,000 for school nursing services each year. We also knew that primary care providers could receive reimbursement directly from health insurance companies and/or Medicaid. Using this knowledge, we created a revenue-based financial model based upon the blending of current dollars spent on school-based nursing and primary care reimbursements from insurance companies and Medicaid. On average, the cost of operating a school-based health center is about $100,000 per school. From this information, we knew that we either had to charge schools more to provide accessible primary care services, or bill insurance companies and Medicaid the equivalent for the difference.

Ultimately, this model was a success. Schools, parents, and insurance companies supported the model, as the alternative was poor health outcomes, students performing poorly in school, and students using costly emergency room visits as primary care. After seven years of operation, health insurance companies and Medicaid are billed for about 25% of associated costs, and schools pay for the remaining 75%. Although financially self-sustainable, the model continues to depend upon philanthropy to fund some infrastructure and new school start-up costs.

Although incorporated as a nonprofit, philanthropically-funded organization, the start-up stage of this model operated within a for-profit business model. If the health insurance reimbursement percentage can be increased through increased utilization, the model will eventually demonstrate profits and surpluses.

Stage Four: SCALING AND SCALING IMPACT & SYSTEM AND POLICY INFLUENCE

Once the first two school models demonstrated to be effective, the model quickly scaled to approximately 20 charter and private schools within the region, and continues to grow within that category.

To reach significant scale, the model informed the development of a Request For Proposals released by the School District of Philadelphia. They aimed to build a larger model which could leverage healthcare dollars in order to achieve better health and education outcomes across the district. As this model has great scaling potential, overhead costs would decrease significantly, and potentially expand in similar ways to the retail clinic model.

This model has been published, and has the potential for being replicated by other providers (i.e. Federally Qualified Health Centers) in other states. The reason that Federally Qualified Health Centers are targeted for replication is that they receive an enhanced reimbursement rate that ensures the model is financially sustainable.

Stage Five: EXECUTION STRATEGY

In order to execute this model, we needed respected individuals to support us from within the education and healthcare industries. Fortunately, Nick was able to open doors and initiate contracts with charter schools, and Tine had the healthcare knowledge and relationships necessary to leverage resources in the healthcare industry. It was our combined expertise and networks that allowed the model to launch.

We knew that if we wanted this model to scale, we needed to invest in full-time staff; regardless of the fact that the model was not yet financially self-sustainable. In order to do this, we hired a full-time executive director and supplemented the salary for two years. The expectation was that, after the two-year period, the executive director's salary level became commensurate with the revenues generated from the model.

SUMMARY

While we are excited about the model we created and its outcomes to date, we realize that its proven success does not necessarily mean that it can be scaled or replicated. Both the education and healthcare industries have their own practices in place, and disrupting them is a considerable threat to their stability. Eventually, our hope is that the model will become the standard in urban schools, and that low-income students and families will have access to primary care. The result would be a healthy and educated student body, capable of thriving and learning. In the process, this model would save the public significant sums of money, which would otherwise have been spent on chronic disease management, emergency room visits, and poor student performance.

SOCIAL MOBILITY VIA COLLEGE COMPLETION

Stage One: IDEA FORMULATION AND EXPLORATION

Step 1: Defining our "Why"

The reason we decided to tackle this issue stemmed from the hundreds of thousands of individuals who still believe in the American Dream of making a better life for themselves and their families. After leading a large nonprofit organization dedicated to strengthening a community's ability to become economically self-sufficient, Nick made a sad realization: not only was he not successful, but he never could be. The best that the current system was capable of was keeping impoverished individuals safe. Despite millions of public dollars spent annually within the nonprofit sector and by the agency he ran, funding did not achieve any self-sufficiency for the individuals served. Rather, it trapped people in poverty and created a lifelong dependency on public dollars.

With the belief that everyone can work for self-dignity and pride, we looked for a model that provided a different pathway to financial self-sufficiency.

Stage Two: DESIGN THINKING AND RAPID PROTOTYPING

Step 1: Challenge Conventional Wisdom by Creating New Strategies; Modify the Rules of the Industry

In researching the models that had been proven to work, we learned that most government-funded workforce development programs had high rates of initial job placements. However, many people failed to retain their jobs after three to nine months, and ultimately failed to achieve higher incomes. Even when "successful," the enrolled individuals did not advance on the social mobility scale. The few who had maintained their positions were only able to come off of public benefits because they picked up multiple, low-wage jobs in order to survive. The models that were successful, such as the Greystone Bakery model, created a career path for hard-to-employ individuals by operating a business and employing the individuals themselves. However, the limitation of this model was that it was incapable of scaling; it could only employ and support a small number of individuals based on sales.

Further research revealed that higher education degrees and vocational certificates led to higher rates of sustainable wages. Without an advanced degree or certificate, people become entrenched in poverty. Ironically, however, we also discovered that many individuals are unable to increase their overall income even with a higher wage; as their earning potential increases, their public subsidies decrease at the same rate, ultimately leaving them in the same financial situation. One research study suggests that, in order move out of poverty, an individual with dependents must earn approximately $22 - $25/hour. Only when a person earns the equivalent of this wage can they move from being a dependent to a contributor to society. Unsurprisingly, many of the jobs which pay $22 - $25/hour are those which require an advanced degree or certificate.

The majority of nonprofits dedicated to the higher education pipeline focus on getting students into college. Far fewer focus on tracking the obtainment of a diploma. Without a degree, good intentioned individuals, organizations, and colleges often cause more harm than help; for the students who drop out before obtaining a diploma, they are saddled with crippling student loan debt. This launches the affected individuals further into poverty, and bars them from being able to afford going back to school if they want to try again.

Step 2: Design Thinking and Rapid Prototyping

Rather than creating our own solution, we decided to join forces with a willing academic partner to scale an existing social impact model. I-LEAD, in partnership with Harcum College, enrolls adult, working learners in an accredited Associate's Degree program. Classes are given onsite, and in accessible, local neighborhood buildings (i.e. public schools, churches, libraries, community-based organizations, etc.) during evening hours, in an accelerated cohort-based format. The "real-world" curriculum is developed to complement, rather than complicate the demands of work and family.

The program's unique components of success include:

- *Convenience of time and location*: To accommodate the schedules of working adults, classes take place two evenings per week in close proximity to where students live. Courses are consolidated into four, eight-week mini semesters per academic year, and students earn an Associate's Degree in five to six traditional semesters.

- *Maximum financial aid*: Students achieve full-time status, therefor becoming eligible for a full financial aid package. Low-income students can generally fund 95% of their tuition (priced substantially below average market costs) through financial aid.
- *Maintenance of low cost:* Bringing college directly into the community removes transportation and centralized campus expenses, and leverages underutilized assets of neighborhood institutions to keep costs low.
- *Relevant curriculum:* Curriculum content is relevant to work and life, and builds upon a 21st century skill set sought by employers, including oral and written communication skills, math, information technology, analytical skills, team building, and leadership. The curriculum is taught in a classroom with a teaching style targeted towards adult learners. Students' college level skills are efficiently developed through non-credit, remedial courses taken alongside credit-bearing courses.
- *Size of community higher education schools:* Limiting the student body to 100 - 150 students, per site, facilitates a personalized learning experience.
- *Cohort-based model:* Peer support is critical to success as students journey through the program together in learning cohorts.
- *Student success services:* A single point of contact at the community institution delivers academic and non-academic support services designed to help students navigate the unfamiliar bureaucracy of higher education.

This model demonstrated an 80% graduation rate, which far exceeded the national community college graduation rate of 10 - 15%. Using community-based organizations as partnership sites, this model was able to leverage existing community structures and relationships to great advantage.

Based on this model's success, we began wondering if the model would work well for other target populations (i.e. recent high school graduates, working adults in a corporate setting, and foster care individuals who are transitioning out of the foster care system).

In our attempt to reach recent high school graduates, we garnered enough support to open up three pilot sites in alternative learning environments as well as one site in a charter school. We attempted to initiate this model in public high school sites, but, despite our best efforts with school administration, students never enrolled. The results of the pilot program indicated that a high school setting only worked when it shared attributes of community-based organizations, such as longstanding social relationships with community members. Out of the four alternative education and charter schools sites, one site thrived, two closed, and one transitioned into a community site.

In order to address individuals working in a corporate setting, we launched a site within a large nonprofit organization. This pilot worked with community members who, on average, were making only $12/hour with a high school diploma. By providing an accessible and affordable option to these individuals, many were able to enroll in the alternative college model.

Finally, we addressed the issue of foster care students; only 4% of which attend college. We determined that we needed a site tailored to the needs of foster care students instead of sending them to existing organizations. As a result, we saw an initial cohort of 30 foster care students enrolled in the pilot.

Stage Three: FINANCIAL MODELING AND RAISING START-UP CAPITAL

In order to fund this type of model, we needed to research student financial aid. We quickly learned that low-income individuals can receive between $10,000 and $12,000 in financial aid, per year (depending upon a state's financial aid policy). Both federal and state governments allocate an annual amount of financial aid to students in need. The only institutions that can access financial aid dollars, however, are colleges and universities.

How, then, could we access financial aid dollars? And can a higher education degree be provided at just above what a low-income individual can leverage in financial aid? We learned that colleges are not permitted to outsource their academic (i.e. instructional) components, but they *can* outsource student support services. With this in mind, we needed a college partnership which was driven by a mission to educate low-income, primarily minority, students. In addition, the college needed to be willing to outsource their student support services to organizations which had "social contracts" with these students in order to ensure their success in a college environment. Eventually, we were able to come to an agreement in which 20% of a student's tuition would be paid to the organization to coordinate and hire mentors and coaches for student support services. A key component of this financial model is that the organization is only paid their revenue share if the student achieves success (as defined by passing courses and graduating with a degree). Each student is an investment.

Stage Four: SCALING, SCALING IMPACT, & SYSTEM AND POLICY INFLUENCE
When we tried to scale this model to other colleges and universities, we found that no one was willing to reduce their tuition or share financial aid dollars in order to support low-income students. We were forced to conclude that most college models are not set-up to serve *all* students. Instead, many are designed around the values of exclusivity and high college rankings.

We also realized that not all colleges are governed the same way. Some are allowed to grow and expand freely (i.e. the addition of online courses, satellite sites, new courses, etc.), while other colleges must obtain approval from the Department of Education, which restricts their ability to be innovative and respond to the needs of students.

Our current scaling impact strategy revolves around the expansion of the Harcum College / I-LEAD model to include new target populations (i.e. foster care students and unemployed individuals). Eventually, we hope the success of this model will influence public policy and/or incentivize other colleges to adopt similar models.

Stage Five: EXECUTION STRATEGY

Through execution and expansion, we learned that a partnering organization must have a minimum of six months cash flow in order to support this model. Additionally, the organization must have authentic social relationships with community residents and a dedicated individual to champion the effort. If any of the above components are missing, this model cannot launch or succeed.

It should be noted that this model required champions outside of the official organizations as well. Beyond Harcum College, I-LEAD, and various community centers, we still needed substantial help from other entities to provide the introductions necessary to make and support vital new partnerships.

SUMMARY

Although this model has limited scalability (it currently serves 600 students in the region), it has grown larger than any other workforce development model in the region. Perhaps more importantly, is that this model is also self-sustaining. Eventually, we hope that other colleges will adapt their own models in order to fulfil the mission of serving a low-income target population. Consumers who can no longer afford higher education models will start choosing affordable and accessible models, which will ultimately drive mainstream colleges to adopt similar programs.

EARLY LITERACY FOR CHILDREN WITH LEARNING DIFFERENCES

Stage One: **IDEA FORMULATION AND EXPLORATION**

Step 1: Defining our "Why"

We chose to tackle this issue because it affected each of us personally. Tine's son was attending a high quality, traditional school, but was struggling to learn how to read. After a few years of advocacy and research, her son was diagnosed with double deficit dyslexia, and was placed in a specialized private school. Nick, on the other hand, is a certified elementary teacher, had founded a charter school, and grew up in a home environment dedicated to children and adults with learning differences.

Driven by the frustrating experience of determining why her son was not learning how to read, and then paying the cost of an education tailored towards a child with dyslexia, Tine knew she needed help. After many conversations with Nick, they partnered to find a way to provide accessible and affordable public education options to students with learning differences.

Stage Two: DESIGN THINKING AND RAPID PROTOTYPING

Step 1: Challenging conventional wisdom which modifies the "rules" of the industry

We started this process by researching the industry and understanding current best practices. As a result, we learned that one in five students has a language-based learning disability (National Dissemination Center for Children with Disabilities, 2011). Dyslexia is the most common of the language-based learning disabilities, and affects roughly 10 - 15% of the population. Children with learning disabilities often remain undiagnosed, and are frequently held to the same standards as other students. This results in increased hardship and frustration in school, which leads to higher rates of school dropouts. In turn, the reduced earning potential of dropouts costs the federal government $158 billion or more in lost revenue each year. These children may eventually require other state and federal funding, as well as government-subsidized health and human services assistance. Additionally, children of dropouts are more likely to drop out of school themselves, and fall into a vicious cycle of poverty.

While there are a lot of evidence-based educational programs and services for children with learning disabilities, many of the existing educational services are extremely expensive for parents, who have to pay for educational services out of pocket. The average tuition cost of a specialty private school which focuses on teaching students with learning disabilities is between $25,000 and $40,000 per year. In addition, parents of children with learning disabilities spend between $10,000 and $12,000 per year on private tutors. As traditional educational settings often fail these students, and private schools are often too expensive for parents, alternative learning opportunities are needed to ensure that children with learning disabilities get the support they need.

Step 2: Design Thinking and Rapid Prototyping

We started by talking with our target population: hundreds of parents with children who have learning disabilities. We then created a belief statement that reflected their experiences and what they desired for their children.

> *We believe in the power of PARENTS to educate and guide their children in the learning process. We do this by giving parents the knowledge and tools necessary to decrease their dependence on formal educational systems.*
> *We do this because we know that millions of caring parents have voiced their frustrations on behalf of their children, who are forced into a one-size-fits-all educational system. We do this because we demand an educational system that adapts to a child's learning style, teaches them at their respective academic level, and allows them to pursue their academic passions and interests.*
> *We do this because parents are asking for a roadmap to take control of their child's educational experience.*

This belief statement evolved into an alternative school model driven by two key values: personalized instruction and inquiry-based education.

PERSONALIZED INSTRUCTION: Students are provided with an individualized education path that utilizes their strengths, talents, and interests to ensure a passion for learning. Technology-based platforms ensure students are progressing at their own pace toward achieving subject mastery.

INQUIRY-BASED EDUCATION: Students drive the education process through their interests and passions. Inquiry-based instruction ensures that the educational process is valued, which leads towards the creation of lifelong learners.

Our first attempt at creating a model was driven by affordability, so we became chartered to operate a cyber charter school. The technology required by a cyber school allowed for individualized instruction, which was beneficial to each student's pace and instructional level. As students were able to work independently, technology allowed teachers the freedom to provide specialized instruction to individuals or small groups. While this model demonstrated significant academic gains (i.e. double the average of traditional educational models), it did not ultimately achieve our social impact goals for three reasons:

1. It attracted all types of students (i.e. autistic, low-income, and physically handicapped children) who were seeking alternative educational models. As the school received public dollars, we were required to serve all types of students. While this was beneficial to many, it also meant that the school could not achieve its primary goal of specializing towards its target population.

2. Public education is highly regulated, and a large portion of the budget was dedicated to meet these regulations. This ultimately undermined the model, as it took financial resources away from small student/teacher ratios. Additionally, regulations required teachers to teach to the standards required by the state in lieu of what was needed by the students.

3. Teachers had a challenge partnering with parents, as teachers continued to see this setting as their domain. This meant that they spent their time teaching *for* the parent, instead of teaching *with* the parent. As a result, they stopped adapting the individualized model and tried to fit students into a standardized model.

Taking this new knowledge into consideration, we adapted the model so that it could provide parents directly with the skills and tools they needed to help their children thrive. This required us to create a new prototype and retest the model on our target consumers. To do this, we created customer service prototypes (as seen on the following page) which included an image of the current experience of parents and students, and contrasted it with a "better," alternative model. We then tested these prototypes on hundreds of parents to see if there was real value to our idea. Could this new model be the answer that parents and students were looking for?

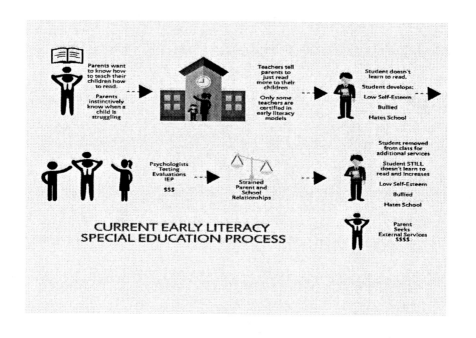

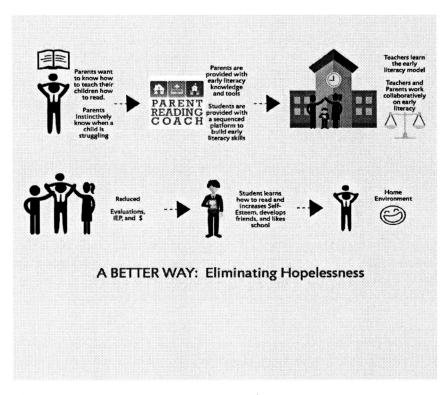

A BETTER WAY: Eliminating Hopelessness

After numerous conversations and adaptations, Parent Reading Coach™ was born. This national company is based upon the premise that all children can read when: parents can use research-informed learning techniques and strategies; every child is valued for his or her uniqueness and is able to learn at his or her respective academic level; and parents shift from delivering content to being facilitators of learning. Parent Reading Coach™ provides training videos and a virtual student platform to caregivers and students. Through this system, vested parents and caregivers have access to the tools and knowledge necessary to help their children learn to read. Parent Reading Coach™ uses a cloud-based platform that can be used to disseminate material to students, parents, and teachers, as well as administer reading-based learning challenges. The program moves sequentially, and prevents students from progressing until they demonstrate mastery through parent engagement. Additionally, this model allows students to build their own skills, and teaches them the foundations of reading by practicing and progressing without relying entirely on their parents and teachers. Finally,

Parent Reading Coach™ has adapted to include the distribution of hardcopy books, as students and parents determined that they needed physical materials in addition to the online platform in order to be successful.

Stage Three: FINANCIAL MODELING AND RAISING START-UP CAPITAL

In looking at our financial model, we began to look into which entities were currently receiving financial revenues to provide similar services to the students. We quickly realized that government organizations (i.e. school districts), government-certified entities (i.e. charter schools), and government-contracted entities (i.e. specialized schools or service providers) were the recipients of public dollars. Tutoring companies, on the other hand, were consumer-driven services.

Our original, cyber charter school model had been based upon direct government sources, which required the approval and charter authorization of the State of Pennsylvania. Once we determined that this system would be unsuccessful for our new model, we determined that a better option might be a financial model built upon consumer demand and indirect government funding.

When building a financial model based upon consumer demand, we needed to ensure that the model was affordable. We therefore created projected revenues and expenses as seen in the table on the following page. This spreadsheet defines periods of profits and losses, and outlines revenues from parent consumers (i.e. subscriptions and coaching); teacher consumers (i.e. certifications); and institutional consumers (i.e. schools).

Parent Reading Coach™ FINANCIAL PROJECTIONS	2016	Oct	Nov	Dec	Jan	Feb	Mar	Apr	May	June	SUMMARY
REVENUES											
Subscriptions ($10/user)	10	0	1000	1000	5000	5000	10000	10000	10000	10000	52010
Parent Coaching ($50/hr)	50	0	0	1250	2500	3750	5000	6250	7500	8750	35050
Certifications ($250/user)	250	0	0	0	2500	5000	5000	0	0	0	12750
Consulting ($1,500/day)	1500	0	0	0	7500	7500	7500	0	0	0	24000
TOTAL		0	1000	2250	17500	21250	27500	16250	17500	18750	122000
EXPENSES											
Development Costs ($100,000)											
Technology Consultants		0	0	0	1000	1000	1000	1500	1500	2000	8000
Parent Coaching		0	0	1250	2500	3750	5000	6250	7500	8750	35000
Certifications		0	0	0	2500	5000	5000	0	0	0	12500
Consulting		0	0	0	7500	7500	7500	0	0	0	22500
Social Marketing Costs		0	5000	5000	5000	5000	5000	5000	5000	5000	40000
TOTAL		0	5000	6250	18500	22250	23500	12750	14000	15750	118000
PROFIT LOSS		0	-4000	-4000	-1000	-1000	4000	3500	3500	3000	4000

Though this model did not include revenue from contract schools, they are still a viable option for funding. The difference between a contract school and a charter school is that a contract school is better able to specialize within a target population, and is contracted to deliver a service under the regulatory oversight of district and charter schools.

Strategy aside, the financial model provides information regarding those who contributed revenue for our services (i.e. school districts and tutoring companies). It also uses existing and consistent funding models instead of relying on philanthropy and limited-time grants.

Stage Four: SCALING, SCALING IMPACT, & SYSTEM AND POLICY INFLUENCE

Close to one in five students in English-speaking countries have a language-based learning disability. Dyslexia is the most common of them, and affects an estimated 10 - 15% of the population. Though Parent Reading Coach™ will initially focus its sales within the United States, there is great potential for future scaling on a global level to include other English-speaking countries.

Parent Reading Coach™ markets directly to parents through Social Media groups, and appeals to the following motivated populations:

1) Homeschoolers and parents of dyslexic students and/or children who struggle with reading and writing
2) Four and five-year-olds in head start and daycare programs
3) Afterschool programs and tutoring programs
4) School districts (public, charter, and private)

Stage Five: EXECUTION STRATEGY

Execution strategy is all about competition, competitive position, and risk assessment. In this example, even though there were existing, evidence-based educational programs and services for children with learning disabilities, many of them were too costly for parents to afford.

Parent Reading Coach™ offers the only evidence-informed, virtual training and early literacy platform for students with learning disabilities. The program is both accessible and affordable, and it is targeted directly towards parents and caregivers. Research shows that this type of learning system offers promising, new ways of learning that could transform those currently labeled as "non-academics" into flourishing, confident self-learners.

Ultimately, Parent Reading Coach™ envisions a world in which all children are literate. This model also pushes for motivated teachers to acquire early literacy training, which is often excluded from their higher education degrees. Parent Reading Coach™ might not ensure literacy for everyone, but it does provide the essential knowledge and tools necessary to eliminate the hopelessness that many parents experience when their child does not fit into the traditional educational system.

SUMMARY

Parent Reading Coach™ continues to evolve based on consumer-driven feedback. For example, as parents seek to reduce the time that their children spend in front of computer screens, Parent Reading Coach™ is adapting to include physical books as part of its curriculum. These books follow the same sequence as the online platform, and meet a current gap in early literacy books in the market place.

CONCLUSION

After discovering your "Why," and working through the five stages of social innovation detailed in this book, you should be well on your way to launching a unique product or service. Ultimately, it is our hope that your social innovation not only improves communities, but serves as a catalyst for others to follow in your footsteps.

There are many complex and challenging issues that must be solved in order to bring about a more peaceful world, and we applaud you for taking the time to learn about yourself, collaborate with likeminded peers, and discover how an entrepreneurial spirit can lead to greater social impact.

We wish you the best on your journey, and we cannot wait to hear about what types of ideas you have cooking up. Please do be in touch, and more importantly, stay true to your dreams, passions, and motivations. It's people like you that make this world a better place.

For updates, contact information, and Social Innovations news, please visit:

www.socialinnovationsinstitute.com

**Does your organization need a Social Innovations Lab Process?
Contact Nicholas D. Torres at nick@socialinnovationspartners.org**

ABOUT THE AUTHORS

Nicholas Torres, M.Ed. has over 20 years of experience in executive management and social innovations. He built and led a nationally recognized human services organization; founded multiple charter schools and nonprofits, and currently leads a social sector think tank organization.

From 2000 – 2010, Mr. Torres served as President of Congreso de Latinos Unidos, where he transformed the organization from a traditional social services agency into a comprehensive, children and family-oriented human services nonprofit. He achieved this by integrating education, behavioral health, and primary healthcare into one service model. Under his leadership, Congreso was awarded one of six national leadership investments from the Edna McConnell Clark Foundation, in recognition of the organization's commitment to young people, aged 16 -24. As a result of this investment, Mr. Torres created an innovative performance management system which measured organizational effectiveness for over 50 service lines and 17,000 clients. Mr. Torres also served as a member of the National Alliance for Effective Social Investments, which led the nation on integrating Social Impact Indicators into nonprofit best practices.

Currently, Mr. Torres serves as the Chief Executive Officer and Co-Founder of Social Innovations Partners, which manages the Social Innovation Journal, Institute, & Lab. He also oversees Parent Reading Coach™, a technology-based Early Literacy Company. Outside of his work with nonprofits, he teaches classes at the University of Pennsylvania's Fels Institute of Government and Wharton School of Business.

Mr. Torres has co-authored several books, and has received multiple advocacy and leadership awards, including the Eisenhower Fellowship, the Business Journal 40 under 40, and Leadership Philadelphia's 101 Connectors.

Mr. Torres received his BA from Carleton College and his Master in Educational Psychology from the University of Texas at Austin.

Tine Hansen-Turton, MGA, JD, FCPP, FAAN is an Executive with more than 20 years of experience in health and human services senior management, executive leadership, and consulting. She founded and led several nationally recognized organizations and trade associations. A proven results-oriented, strategic leader, Ms. Hansen-Turton is known for being an effective organizational change agent, and a successful policy reform advocate.

In October, 2016, Ms. Hansen-Turton was appointed as President and Chief Executive Officer of Woods Services, a $230 million multi-service healthcare and human services organization dedicated to providing innovative and comprehensive services to children and adults with developmental disabilities. Ms. Hansen-Turton is also the founding Executive Administrator for the Convenient Care Association (CCA), a national trade association of more than 2,300 private sector retail clinics, serving nearly 30 million people across the country.

Previously, Ms. Hansen-Turton held positions as the Chief Operating Officer of the Public Health Management Corporation and as the Chief Executive Officer of the National Nurse-led Care Consortium.

To date, Ms. Hansen-Turton has co-authored eight books and currently publishes Philadelphia's Social Innovations Journal. She has received several advocacy and leadership awards, including the prestigious Eisenhower Fellowship, the Business Journal 40 under 40, and the Leadership and Women of Distinction Awards. She was named one of the 101 emerging Philadelphia connectors by Leadership, Inc., and is an American Express NextGen Independent Sector Fellow. Outside of her work in healthcare, she teaches classes at the University of Pennsylvania.

Ms. Hansen-Turton received her BA from Slippery Rock University, her Master of Government and Public Administration from the University of Pennsylvania's Fels Institute of Government, and her Juris Doctor from the Temple University Beasley School of Law.

ADVISORS

David Castro is the Executive Director of I-LEAD; Ashoka, Eisenhower and Kellogg Fellow.
Christopher Creswell is Owner and Manager of New Enterprise Ventures.
Peter Hotz is Founder and Manager of 5Cap Ventures.
Heather Falck is the Manager of the Independence Blue Cross Foundation.
William J. Greene is a Member of Green Law PLLC, Founder Homestead Smart Health Plans and SRC.
David Griffith is the E.D. of Episcopal Community Services and Chairman of Modern Group Ltd.
Karin Annerhed-Harris is the Associate Director of the Alliance of Community Service Providers.
Jeff Hornstein is the Director of Financial & Policy Analysis, Philadelphia Controller.
Kevin Leigh is Senior Director at BNY Mellon Wealth Management.
Gavin Kerr is President and CEO of Inglis.
Laura Kind McKenna is a Trustee of the Patricia Kind Family Foundation.
John Moore is Executive Chairman of Impact PHL & the Managing Partner of Robin Hood Ventures.
Joseph Pyla is the President of the Thomas J. Scattergood Behavioral Health Foundation.
Sandy Festa Ryan is Vice President, Walmart Care Clinics.
Donald Tretola is Senior Vice President of Public Affairs & Program Dev. for Allies, NJ.
Steve Tremitiere is Founder and CEO of GrayHare Ventures.

Does your organization need a Social Innovations Lab Process?
Contact Nicholas D. Torres at nick@socialinnovationspartners.org